101 Ways to Eat Macaroni and Cheese

A Guide for the
Poor and Starving
College Student!
(And Everyone Else on a Budget)

Andrew Mann

PublishAmerica
Baltimore

First printing

ISBN: 1-4137-7051-7
PUBLISHED BY PUBLISHAMERICA, LLLP
www.publishamerica.com
Baltimore

Printed in the United States of America

Over the years, I noticed that I have something in common with just about every single person in college or university who was living on a shoestring budget—our lives seemed to revolve around macaroni and cheese.

It was a choice dictated by necessity. In fact, as I talked about this time of my life with friends, I often joked that I was an expert in cooking macaroni and cheese and could very easily write a book with over a 101 ways to prepare it. At first, it was meant as a joke, but over time I realized that this was something that I could do. What struck me was how this part of my life was almost universal with all the students or former students that I talked to.

I even went to the effort to buy some cookbooks at the university bookstore, but somehow I always came back to my favorite pasta due to finances or lack of skill! I always believed that if I had a book that could put all the macaroni and cheese recipes into some resemblance of order, my life in the kitchen would have been much less stressful and more organized.

The reason that I gravitated to macaroni and cheese, or any recipe involving macaroni, was simple. I could always go to the local store and get several boxes or packages for very little money. By adding a little of this and that, I had a completely different meal each time, whether it was cooked in a pot, used in a casserole or in a salad. Just altering a few key ingredients can give you an entirely different dish! The most important thing to me, other than how cheap it was to make, was it could be wrapped in a sealed container and eaten later on in the day and in coming days—hot or cold!

The purpose of this book is to put together 101 recipes from family and friends that I have collected over the course of my travels to make life easier for those who are on a budget but still want to cook something that is fast, easy, and will impress friends and family. Plain old macaroni and cheese gets to be boring after a while, but with these recipes, I think you will find that this pasta is much more versatile than given credit for, and that you can still watch your budget but have a classy and versatile meal!

101 Ways to Eat Macaroni and Cheese

3-Cheeses Macaroni and Cheese

16 ounces elbow macaroni
1 stick butter or margarine
salt and pepper
8 ounces grated mild cheddar cheese
8 ounces grated sharp cheddar cheese
8 ounces grated Velveeta brand cheese
2 eggs, beaten
1 can evaporated milk
paprika

– Boil macaroni and drain and put into a 4-quart baking dish.
– Add butter or margarine.
– Add salt and pepper to taste then add cheese to macaroni.
– Add eggs and milk then sprinkle paprika on top of macaroni and cheese.
– Bake at 350 degrees till browned.

Serves 4-6

2

3-Cheeses Macaroni and Cheese (Version 2.0)

1 pound macaroni noodles
4 tablespoons butter
1/3 cup flour
4 cups milk
1 teaspoon salt
freshly ground black pepper
1 dash hot sauce
3 cups grated cheddar cheese
1/2 cup grated mild cheese
1/4 cup grated Parmesan cheese

– Cook pasta according to packet instructions, drain and set aside.
– Heat oven to 350 degrees.
– In a saucepan over medium heat, melt butter and stir in flour to form a paste then slowly mix in milk.
– Bring to a simmer, constantly stirring over low heat, until sauce begins to thicken.
– Season with salt, pepper and the hot sauce.
– Remove from stove and stir in 1 1/2 cups of the cheddar cheese until it is blended.
– Butter a 4-quart baking dish.
– Layer pasta, remaining tasty cheddar and mild cheese, and sauce.
– Sprinkle the top with Parmesan.
– Bake 30 minutes until bubbly and golden.

SERVES 4-6

3

4-Cheese Macaroni

1/3 cup flour
2 2/3 cups milk
3 ounces Swiss cheese, shredded
1/2 cup Parmesan cheese, grated
1/2 cup cheddar cheese, shredded
3 ounces American cheese, cubed
6 cups cooked macaroni
1/4 teaspoon salt
vegetable cooking spray
1/3 cup bread crumbs
1 tablespoon butter, softened

– Preheat oven to 375 degrees.
– Place flour in a large saucepan then gradually add an equal amount of milk, stirring until smooth.
– Add remaining milk, stirring constantly.
– Cook over medium heat until thick and creamy, stirring constantly.
– Add cheeses and cook until cheese melts, stirring often.
– Remove from heat; stir in macaroni and salt.
– Spoon mixture into a 2-quart casserole dish coated with cooking spray.
– In a small bowl, combine bread crumbs and butter and stir until well-blended.
– Sprinkle over macaroni mixture.
– Bake until bubbly and lightly browned, about 30 minutes.

SERVES 4-6

AUTUMN'S MACARONI AND CHEESE

1 pound small elbow macaroni
boiling salt water
1/2 cup butter or margarine
1 cup milk
4 cups shredded sharp cheddar cheese
1/4 teaspoon paprika
salt and pepper

– Follow package directions and cook macaroni in a large pot of boiling salted water.
– Drain thoroughly and melt butter in pot over medium-high heat.
– Add milk, drained macaroni, cheese and paprika..
– Cook, stirring until cheese is melted.

SERVES 4

5

BACON WITH MACARONI AND CHEESE

2 slices bacon
8 ounces penne pasta
1 onion, chopped
1 clove garlic, minced
3 cups shredded cheddar cheese
2 tablespoons butter
3 tablespoons all-purpose flour
2 cups milk

– Preheat oven to 350 degrees.
– Place bacon in a large, deep skillet and cook over medium-high heat until evenly brown.
– Drain, crumble and set aside.
– In a large pot with boiling salted water, cook pasta then drain.
– In a medium skillet, cook the chopped onion and minced garlic.
– Take off heat and add chopped cooked bacon and set aside.
– For the sauce, in a medium saucepan melt the butter or margarine over low heat.
– Once melted, add the flour and stir constantly for 2 minutes.
– Gradually add milk and continue stirring until thickened.
– Stir in 2 cups of the grated cheddar cheese and stir until melted.
– Combine cooked pasta, cooked vegetables and sauce.
– Pour into a 2-quart casserole dish and add the last cup of grated cheddar cheese to top of mixture.
– Bake uncovered in preheated oven until cheese on top is melted and brown, 15 to 20 minutes. Serve warm.

SERVES 5

6

BAKED MACARONI AND CHEESE II

1/2 pound elbow macaroni
3 tablespoons butter
3 tablespoons flour
1 tablespoon powdered mustard
3 cups milk
1/2 cup yellow onion, finely diced
1 bay leaf
1/2 teaspoon paprika
1 large egg
12 ounces sharp cheddar, shredded
1 teaspoon kosher salt
fresh black pepper
3 tablespoons butter
1 cup panko bread crumbs

– Preheat oven to 350 degrees.
– Boil macaroni in lightly salted water until tender then drain.
– In a separate pot, melt the butter.
– Mix in the flour and mustard and stir continuously for five minutes while making sure it's free of lumps.
– Stir in the milk, onion, bay leaf, and paprika and let it simmer for ten minutes and remove the bay leaf.
– Add in the egg then stir in 3/4 of the cheese. Season with salt and pepper.
– Add the macaroni into the mix and pour into a 2-quart casserole dish then top with remaining cheese.
– Melt the butter in a nonstick fry pan and add the bread crumbs to coat.
– Top the macaroni with the bread crumbs. Bake for 30 minutes.

SERVES 6

7

BAKED MACARONI AND CHEESE III

3 tablespoons unsalted butter
3 1/2 tablespoons all-purpose flour
1/2 teaspoon paprika
3 cups milk
1 teaspoon salt
3/4 pound macaroni (rotelle)
1 tablespoon Worcestershire sauce
10 ounces extra-sharp cheddar cheese, shredded coarse
1 cup coarse fresh bread crumbs

– Preheat oven to 375 degrees.
– Add butter to a 2-quart shallow baking dish.
– In a 6-quart kettle, bring 5 quarts salted water to a boil for cooking macaroni.
– In a heavy saucepan, melt butter over moderately low heat and stir in flour and paprika. Lightly cook, mixing 3 minutes, then mix in the milk and salt.
– Bring sauce to a boil, then put to simmer, stirring occasionally for 3 minutes. Remove pan from heat.
– Stir pasta into kettle of boiling water and boil, stirring occasionally, until tender.
– Drain macaroni in a colander and rinse under cold water.
– In a large bowl, stir together pasta, sauce, Worcestershire sauce and 2 cups cheddar then transfer the mixture to prepared dish.
– In a small bowl, toss remaining 3/4 cup cheddar with bread crumbs and sprinkle over the macaroni mixture.
– Bake in the oven 25 to 30 minutes, or until it is golden and bubbling

SERVES 4-6

Baked Macaroni and Cheese
with a Personal Touch

3 cups macaroni
1/2 cup sunflower seeds
1 tablespoon oil
3 tablespoons butter
1 small chopped onion
1 cup sliced mushrooms
2 1/2 cups grated cheddar cheese
1/4 teaspoon nutmeg
1/2 teaspoon paprika
1/2 teaspoon salt
Black pepper to taste
3 cups dry bread crumbs
2 tablespoons butter, melted
1/4 cup chopped bell pepper or fresh parsley as garnish

– Heat oven to 350 degrees.
– Toast sunflower seeds in oil in a skillet until golden and season with a sprinkle of salt.
– Boil macaroni for half the required time (3-4 minutes); the macaroni should still have a definite chew to it. It will continue to cook in the oven.
– Lightly cook the onions until light golden in color then add mushrooms, then continue to lightly cook for another 4 minutes.
– Stir all ingredients together and spoon into a greased baking dish.
– Bake for 20 minutes and cover with bread crumbs.
– Bake another 10 minutes. Garnish with raw green bell pepper or parsley.

SERVES 4-6

९

Baked Macaroni with Tomatoes

1 pound macaroni
1 can condensed cream of cheddar cheese soup (11 ounces)
1 1/2 cups milk
14 ounces extra-sharp white cheddar cheese, shredded, divided
1 can stewed tomatoes (14.5 ounces)
1/4 cup dry bread crumbs

– Boil macaroni in lightly salted water until tender then drain.
– In a large saucepan over low heat, warm soup and add milk then stir.
– Add 1/4 of cheese to soup and remove mixture from heat when cheese is melted.
– Preheat oven to 400 degrees.
– Add macaroni and tomatoes to soup and stir then pour into a 9x13-inch baking dish.
– Cover with bread crumbs and the remaining cheese.
– Bake in preheated oven for 25 to 40 minutes or until the cheese is melted and browned.

Serves 4-6

10

Beef and Cheese Bake

8 ounces macaroni, uncooked
1 pound ground chuck
1/2 cup chopped onion
1 envelope cheese sauce mix (1 1/4 ounces)
1 1/4 cups milk
1/4 cup mayonnaise
1 can chopped mild green chiles (4 ounces)
1 tablespoon butter
1/4 cup fine dry bread crumbs
2 teaspoons dried parsley flakes

– Boil macaroni in lightly salted water until tender then drain.
– In a large skillet, brown ground beef with onion, stirring to break up.
– Drain off excess fat then stir in dry cheese sauce mix, milk, and mayonnaise.
– Add chiles and cooked macaroni and bring to a boil, then stir occasionally.
– Spoon macaroni mixture into a 1 1/2-quart casserole.
– Melt the butter, stir in crumbs and parsley flakes then sprinkle over the casserole.
– Bake at 375 degrees for 20 to 30 minutes, or until lightly browned.

Serves 4-6

Beefy Macaroni and Cheese Bake

1 1/2 cups elbow macaroni
1 pound lean ground beef
1 onion, chopped
1 can crushed tomatoes (14 ounces)
1/2 teaspoon dried thyme
1/2 teaspoon dried oregano
1/2 teaspoon salt
fresh ground pepper
2 tablespoons flour
1 1/2 cups milk
1cup grated cheddar cheese

– Preheat oven to 375 degrees.
– Boil macaroni in lightly salted water until tender then drain.
– In large frying pan, lightly cook beef until browned.
– Add onions and lightly cook until soft and transparent.
– Add tomatoes, thyme, oregano, salt and pepper to taste.
– When macaroni is cooked and drained, add to tomato mixture.
– Simmer, stirring occasionally for about 5 minutes.
– In saucepan, combine milk and flour until it is smooth.
– Cook and stir over medium heat until mixture comes to a boil.
– Turn heat to low and stir in 3/4 cup of the cheese.
– Combine macaroni/meat mixture and cheese sauce. Pour in baking dish.
– Top with remaining cheese.
– Bake until cheese melts and casserole is hot, about 15 to 20 minutes.

Serves 4

12

MACARONI AND CHEESE AND BEEF CASSEROLE WITH THYME

2 1/2 cups uncooked elbow macaroni
1/2 pound ground beef
1 onion, chopped
2 tablespoons white wine
1 1/2 cups milk
1 tablespoon whole grain mustard
1 teaspoon Worcestershire sauce
1/2 teaspoon salt
1/2 teaspoon ground black pepper
1/8 teaspoon cayenne pepper
1/2 cup all-purpose flour
2 1/2 cups shredded sharp cheddar cheese, divided
1 tablespoon chopped fresh thyme
2 cups quartered cherry tomatoes

– Preheat oven to 350 degrees.
– Lightly grease a large casserole dish.
– Bring a large pot of water to a boil.
– Boil macaroni in lightly salted water until tender then drain. Transfer to the prepared casserole dish.
– In a skillet over medium heat, cook and stir the ground beef and onion until beef is evenly brown and onion is tender.
– Stir in the wine and continue cooking 1 minute.
– Mix in the milk, mustard, and Worcestershire sauce.
– Season with salt, pepper, and cayenne pepper.
– Continue to cook and stir until heated through.

- Mix the flour into the skillet, and gradually stir in 2 cups cheese until melted
- Mix in the thyme and cherry tomatoes.
- Stir the skillet mixture into the casserole dish with the macaroni.
- Top with remaining cheese.
- Cook uncovered 30 minutes in the preheated oven, until bubbly and lightly brown.

SERVES 4-6

13

A Big Family Reunion Macaroni and Cheese

3/4 cup butter
1/4 cup minced onions
1 cup flour
1 teaspoon salt
1 1/2 teaspoons dry mustard
2 teaspoons powdered ginger
2 quarts milk
2 teaspoons Worcestershire sauce
2 pounds sharp cheddar cheese, cut in small pieces, finely sliced, coarsely shredded or grated
2 pounds elbow macaroni

– Preheat the oven to 400 degrees.
– Melt butter in 3-quart or larger kettle. Lightly cook onion in butter until soft.
– Add flour mixed with salt, mustard, and ginger, and cook, stirring constantly until bubbly.
– Remove from heat, add milk, stirring continuously.
– Put back on heat and continue stirring until sauce thickens.
– Remove from heat, stir in Worcestershire sauce and cheese, and stir until cheese is melted.
– Mix with macaroni boiled in lightly salted water until tender.
– Bake in the oven in two buttered 11X15 shallow pans,or three buttered 2-quart casseroles, or two 3-quart casseroles.
– Bake uncovered for 20 minutes, then covered for an additional 15-20 minutes.

Serves 20-25

Broccoli with Macaroni and Cheese

8 ounces elbow macaroni
1 cup broccoli florets, fresh or frozen
4 tablespoons butter
2 tablespoons flour
2 cups low-fat (1%) milk
1 cup shredded sharp chedder cheese
1/2 cup shredded Gruyere cheese
1/4 cup grated Parmesan cheese
1/2 teaspoon salt
1/4 teaspoon cayenne pepper
1/4 cup whole-wheat bread crumbs.

– In a medium saucepan, cook macaroni according to package directions and drain.
– Fill another saucepan 3/4 full with water and boil then add broccoli. Reduce heat to medium and cook until slightly firm. Drain and set aside.
– Preheat oven to 375 degrees.
– Grease an 8x8-inch glass baking dish.
– In a medium saucepan, melt butter and add flour, stirring 1 minute, until smooth. Gradually mix in milk, stirring continually until thickened, about 3 minutes, then remove from heat.
– Reserve 1/2 cup cheddar cheese but stir in the remaining cheddar, Gruyere, Parmesan, salt, and cayenne into sauce until all cheeses melt.
– Add macaroni and broccoli to sauce and pour into prepared baking dish.
– Bake 15 minutes then sprinkle top with reserved cheddar and bread crumbs.
– Bake 10 to 15 minutes, until bubbly

Serves 4-6

15

Macaroni and Cheese Carbonara

3 1/4 cups large elbow macaroni (about 11 ounces)
12 bacon slices, chopped
3 cups fresh coarse bread crumbs made from French bread (about 4 ounces)
1 cup (packed) finely grated Parmesan cheese (about 4 ounces)
1/2 cup chopped fresh Italian parsley
2 garlic cloves, minced
3 tablespoons all-purpose flour
6 cups whole milk
6 large egg yolks
1 1/2 teaspoons salt
3/4 teaspoon ground black pepper
3 1/2 cups (packed) grated Fontina cheese (about 14 ounces)
1 1/4 cups frozen peas

– Preheat oven to 350 degrees.
– Butter 13x9x2-inch baking dish.
– Boil macaroni in lightly salted water until tender then drain and rinse under cold water.
– Cook bacon in heavy large pot over medium heat until crisp for 10 minutes.
– Transfer bacon and 1/4 cup pan drippings to large bowl.
– Add bread crumbs, 1/4 cup Parmesan cheese and 1/4 cup parsley to bacon then mix.
– Add minced garlic to remaining pan drippings in pot and lightly cook over medium heat until fragrant for 30 seconds.
– Add flour and mix for 3 minutes then gradually mix in whole milk, then egg yolks, salt and pepper.

- Cook until the mixture thickens, mixing constantly for 12 minutes.
- Add 2 cups Fontina cheese and remaining 3/4 cup Parmesan cheese and mix until cheeses melt then remove from heat.
- Mix in peas, macaroni and remaining 1/4 cup parsley.
- Stir in remaining 1 1/2 cups Fontina. Transfer macaroni mixture to prepared dish.
- Bake macaroni mixture, covered, at 350 degrees until just heated through, for 30 minutes.
- Sprinkle bread crumb mixture over macaroni mixture. Bake just until topping is golden, about 15 minutes. Let stand 15 minutes before serving.

SERVES 8

16

Canadian-Style Macaroni and Cheese

2 cups whole wheat or 100% durum macaroni
1 medium container 2% cottage cheese
3 cups fresh or frozen vegetables, diced
2 cups liquid milk
1/2 cup powdered milk
1/3 cup whole wheat flour
3 tablespoons freshly grated Parmesan or Romano cheese
2 tablespoons peanut oil
1/2 teaspoon dried thyme
1/2 teaspoon dried basil
1/2 teaspoon ground oregano
1/8 teaspoon ground black pepper
1/2 cup whole wheat bread crumbs or toasted wheat germ
1 tablespoon peanut or sesame oil
1 tablespoon freshly grated Parmesan or Romano cheese

– Cook the macaroni in boiling unsalted water until soft when tasted.
– Mix the liquid milk and dry milk together in a medium bowl.
– Blend the flour and oil in a nonstick frying pan and cook over medium-low heat, stirring until it is foamy and dark brown in color.
– Then gradually mix in the milk, 1/4 cup at a time. Keep stirring until the sauce has thickened then add the Parmesan cheese and spices.
– Rinse the cottage cheese in a sieve under cold running water.
– In a large bowl, combine the macaroni, cottage cheese, sauce, and vegetables and pour into a 2-quart lightly greased casserole dish.
– Mix the topping ingredients and spread evenly over the macaroni and cheese. Bake at 350 degrees for 40 to 50 minutes.

Serves 6

17

Tuna Casserole with Cashews

3/4 cup elbow macaroni
1 cup sour cream
1/4 teaspoon ground oregano
2 cans (approximately 7 ounces each) tuna, drained and flaked
1/4 cup sliced black olives
1/4 cup chopped green bell pepper
1/2 cup unsalted cashews
1 1/2 teaspoons seasoned salt
1/4 teaspoon pepper
1 cup shredded sharp cheddar cheese

– Preheat the oven at 350 degrees.
– Boil macaroni in lightly salted water until tender then drain.
– In a large bowl, mix the macaroni, sour cream, ground oregano, tuna, sliced olives, bell pepper, cashews, seasoned salt and pepper and mix well.
– Transfer to a shallow 1 1/2-quart or 2-quart baking dish.
– Sprinkle with the shredded cheese.
– Bake in the oven for 25 minutes

SERVES 4-6

18

CARIBBEAN MACARONI AND CHEESE

8 ounces elbow macaroni, cooked
1 tablespoon onion, finely chopped
1 tablespoon green pepper
1 can evaporated milk
1 tablespoon celery, finely chopped
6 ounces cheddar cheese
dash of pepper
salt to taste

– Boil the macaroni in salt water with the onion, green pepper and celery, stirring every few minutes.
– Add one half of the cheese and stir over low heat until it is melted.
– Season and stir in the evaporated milk.
– Spoon into a well-greased baking pan and sprinkle remaining cheese evenly over the top.
– Bake in a preheated oven at 350 degrees for 20 minutes.

19

CHICKEN AND RANCH SALAD

1 pound macaroni, cooked
1 cup chopped cooked chicken breast
4 cups frozen mixed vegetables, thawed
1/4 cup shredded Cheddar cheese
1 cup ranch salad dressing

– In a large bowl, mix the macaroni, chicken, vegetables, cheese and dressing
– Chill for 20 minutes and serve.

SERVES 8

20

CHILI CASSEROLE WITH MACARONI AND CHEESE

1/2 pound macaroni, cooked
1 can chili with beans (15 ounces)
1 can sweet corn, drained (15 ounces)
1/2 pound ground beef, browned and drained
2 tablespoons hot sauce
1/2 cup chopped onion
1 tablespoon chili seasoning mix
1/2 cup shredded mozzarella cheese

– Preheat oven to 300 degrees.
– In a large bowl, combine the macaroni, chili, corn, beef, hot sauce, onion, seasoning mix and cheese.
– Mix well and spread mixture into a 9x13-inch baking dish.
– Bake in the oven for 20 minutes or until heated through.

SERVES 6

21

CORN WITH MACARONI AND CHEESE CASSEROLE

1 can creamed corn (14.75 ounces)
1 can corn (11.25 ounces)
1 cup macaroni
1/2 cup butter
8 ounces cubed processed cheese food

– Mix together creamed corn, whole kernel corn, and uncooked macaroni.
– Slice the butter or margarine and mix into the corn mixture along with the cheese.
– Place in a buttered casserole dish and cover.
– Bake at 350 degrees for 30 minutes.
– Uncover, stir, and bake uncovered for 30 additional minutes.

SERVES 6

22

CREAM CHEESE AND MACARONI

8 ounces corkscrew macaroni
1/2 cup butter or margarine
1 package cream cheese (8 ounces)
1/4 cup oil
garlic powder
2/3 cup boiling water
1 "shake" of parsley

– Cook the macaroni in salt water then drain.
– Add butter or margarine, cream cheese, oil, garlic and water and mix well until cream cheese dissolves.
– Shake parsley on top.

SERVES 4

23

CHEESY CHICKEN AND MACARONI CASSEROLE

1 package macaroni and cheese
1 can cream of chicken soup
2 to 3 cups cubed, cooked chicken
1 tablespoon of olive oil
1 small onion
1/2 cup chopped celery
2 tablespoons chopped roasted red pepper or pimiento
1 cup frozen mixed vegetables, thawed
buttered bread crumbs (about 2 slices of bread, crumbled and tossed, with about 2 to 3 teaspoons of melted butter)

– Boil macaroni in lightly salted water until tender then drain.
– Stir in cream of chicken soup and chicken.
– In a skillet, lightly cook the onion and celery in oil until softened.
– Add mixed vegetables and red pepper or pimiento.
– Combine with macaroni and cheese mixture then spoon into a lightly buttered casserole dish.
– Top chicken pasta casserole with buttered bread crumbs.
– Bake at 350 degrees for 30 to 40 minutes.

SERVES 4-6

24

CREAMY MACARONI AND CHEESE

2 cups elbow macaroni
4 ounces shredded reduce-fat Monterey Jack cheese
1 cup nonfat cottage cheese
3/4 cup nonfat sour cream
1/3 cup skim milk
1/4 cup chopped onions
1 egg white, lightly beaten
1 tablespoon light margarine, melted
1 tablespoon cheese-flavored granules
1 teaspoon dry mustard
1/4 teaspoon black pepper
pinch of ground red pepper
2 tablespoons reduced-fat butter-flavored cracker crumbs
1/2 teaspoon paprika

– Coat a 2-quart casserole dish with nonstick spray.
– Boil macaroni in lightly salted water until tender then drain, reserving two tablespoons of the cooking water.
– Mix the macaroni with reserved cooking water, cheeses, sour cream, milk, onions, egg white, margarine, cheese-flavored granules, mustard and peppers until well combined.
– Spoon into the casserole dish, sprinkle with cracker crumbs and paprika then cover.
– Bake casserole at 350 degrees for 25 minutes.
– Uncover and bake until golden brown and bubbly, about five minutes.

SERVES 4

25

CREAMY MUSHROOM MACARONI AND CHEESE

1 package elbow macaroni (16 ounces)
1 tablespoon butter
1/3 cup milk
1 can condensed cream of mushroom soup (10.75 ounces)
1 pound processed cheese food, cubed

- Boil the macaroni in salted water until it is cooked then drain.
- Preheat the oven to 350 degrees.
- In medium saucepan over medium heat, combine butter, milk, mushroom soup and processed cheese.
- Stir until the cheese is melted and mixture is smooth then stir in the cooked pasta.
- Pour into 2-quart baking dish and bake 20 minutes or until top is golden brown.

SERVES 4-6

26

Chicken Macaroni and Cheese

4 cups chicken broth
2 slices bacon, cut up
1/3 cup finely chopped onion
2 cups shredded American cheese
1 package frozen green peas, cooked and drained (10 ounces)
3 tablespoons sherry
8 ounces elbow macaroni, uncooked
1/4 cup finely chopped green pepper
2 cups cooked chicken, cut up
1/4 cup chopped pimiento

– In a saucepan, heat chicken broth until it is boiling.
– Add the macaroni and cook until tender; do not drain.
– In a large skillet, fry bacon until crisp then add green pepper and onion.
– Cook and stir until onion is tender then drain excess fat.
– Stir in macaroni-broth mixture and the remaining ingredients.

Serves 6-8

27

CHILES AND MACARONI AND CHEESE

6 cups cooked macaroni
2 packages cheese sauce mix
1 can green chiles, whole or diced
1 medium onion, diced
3 cups shredded cheddar cheese
3/4 cups milk
1 cube butter

– Boil the macaroni in salt water until tender then put into a casserole dish.

– In a medium sauce pan, make cheese sauce according to package directions. Add 1 cup of cheese and diced green chiles.

– In a small frying pan, cook the onion in butter until transparent then add it to the cheese sauce.

– Add cheese sauce mix to macaroni and mix.

– Top with the green chiles and the remaining cheese. Bake at 350 degrees for 30 minutes.

SERVES 6

28

College Student's Gourmet Pasta

16 ounces elbow macaroni
2 tablespoons butter
1/2 teaspoon garlic salt
1/4 cup milk
2 tablespoons Parmesan cheese

– Cook macaroni in boiling salted water until tender then drain.
– In a saucepan, add butter or margarine, salt, milk, and Parmesan cheese.
– Cook over low heat until combined.
– Pour mixture over pasta and serve.

SERVES 6

29

CREAMY MACARONI AND CHEESE

1/2 pound elbow macaroni
4 tablespoons (1/2 stick) butter, cut into bits
tabasco sauce
1 12-ounce can evaporated milk (or use whole milk mixed with a little cream)
2 eggs, beaten
1 teaspoon dry mustard, dissolved in a little water
1 pound sharp cheddar cheese, grated
salt and freshly ground pepper

– Preheat oven to 350 degrees.
– Boil the macaroni in salt water until it is tender. Drain and toss into the butter in a large, ovenproof mixing bowl.
– Mix a dash of tabasco into the evaporated milk.
– Reserving about 1/3 cup, stir the milk into the macaroni, then add the eggs, mustard, and 3/4 of the cheese.
– When well combined, season to taste with salt and pepper, and set the bowl directly in the oven.
– Every five minutes, remove it briefly to stir in some of the reserved cheese, adding more evaporated milk as necessary to keep the mixture moist and smooth.
– When all the cheese has been incorporated and the mixture is nicely hot and creamy, then serve.

SERVES 6

30

Custard Macaroni and Cheese

1/2 pound macaroni
1 tablespoon butter
1 egg, beaten
1 teaspoon dry mustard
3 cups grated sharp cheddar cheese
1 cup milk

– Boil macaroni in lightly salted water until tender then drain.
– Stir in butter and egg.
– Mix mustard and salt with 1 tablespoon of hot water then add to the milk.
– Add 3/4 of the cheese to milk.
– Pour macaroni into a buttered casserole and add the milk/cheese mixture.
– Sprinkle top with the remaining cheese.
– Bake at 350 degrees for approximately 40 minutes, or until the custard is set and top is crusty.

SERVES 4

31

CROCK-POT MACARONI AND CHEESE WITH HAM

1 center-cut ham slice, about 12 to 16 ounces, diced
1 rib celery, chopped
1 tablespoon minced dried onion, or use chopped fresh onion
2 teaspoons dried parsley
1 teaspoon celery seed
1 package Kraft Classic Melts Cheddar-American shredded cheese or
an American process cheese (8 ounces)
1 can condensed cream of celery soup, undiluted (10 3/4 ounces)
1 can diced tomatoes with juice
1 cup frozen mixed vegetables (peas, carrots, green beans), thawed
black pepper to taste
5 to 6 cups hot cooked elbow macaroni

– Combine all ingredients, except the mixed vegetables and macaroni, in the slow cooker or Crock-Pot.
– Cover and cook on low for 6 to 7 hours.
– Add vegetables about 1 hour before serving.
– Cook macaroni in salt water until tender and drain.
– Pour Crock-Pot mixture into a large serving bowl then mix the macaroni into it and stir thoroughly.

SERVES 4-6

32

CUSTARD-STYLE MACARONI AND CHEESE

2 quarts water
1 1/2 cups macaroni
2 teaspoons salt
3 large eggs
1 1/2 cups milk
1 teaspoon salt
1/2 teaspoon paprika
2 pinches ground red (cayenne) pepper
1 1/2 cups grated cheese
1/4 cup Parmesan cheese
5 saltine crackers (1/4 cup, crumbled)

– Cook the macaroni in a large pot of salted water and boil until tender.

– Rinse thoroughly in cold water and drain then refrigerate until ready to use.

– Preheat the oven to 325 degrees. Grease a 10x6x2-inch casserole dish.

– Prepare the custard. In a mixing bowl, mix together the eggs, milk, salt, paprika, and ground red pepper.

– In the casserole dish, layer the cooked macaroni with the cheese, and pour the custard over the top and bake for 40 minutes, or until set in the center.

– In a small mixing bowl, combine the Parmesan cheese and crumbled crackers. Spread over the casserole, and broil to brown.

SERVES 5

33

DEEP DESIRES MACARONI AND CHEESE

1 package elbow macaroni (16 ounces)
1 1/2 pounds ground beef
1 tablespoon vegetable oil
1 large onion, chopped
2 cloves garlic, chopped
1 can stewed tomatoes, undrained (14 ounces)
1 jar spaghetti sauce (16 ounces)
1 can mushroom stems and pieces, undrained (12 ounces)
2 cups sour cream
1 pound Colby-Monterey Jack cheese, shredded

– Preheat oven to 350 degrees.
– Cook macaroni in a large pot of lightly salted water and boil until it is tender then drain.
– Place ground beef in a large deep skillet and cook over medium-high heat until evenly brown and crumbled.
– Drain excess fat and set aside.
– Heat oil in a large heavy skillet over medium heat. Cook onion until soft and transparent.
– Stir in garlic and cook for 30 seconds then add cooked beef, tomatoes, spaghetti sauce and mushrooms. Bring to a boil.
– Reduce heat and simmer 20 minutes.
– In a 9x13-inch casserole dish, layer 1/2 of the pasta, 1/2 of the meat sauce, 1/2 of the sour cream and 1/2 of the shredded cheese. Repeat layers.
– Cover and bake in preheated oven for 45 minutes.

SERVES 6

34

DEEP-FRIED MACARONI AND CHEESE

1 package Stouffer's Family-Style Recipes Macaroni & Cheese
fresh crumbs made from plain white bread

– Remove macaroni and cheese from the freezer and, while still frozen, scoop into balls about 1 1/2 inches in diameter.
– Roll balls in bread crumbs.
– Place balls on a cookie sheet or tray and refreeze 10 to 15 minutes.
– Preheat oil in deep fryer to 350 .
– To fry, use tongs or a long-handled spoon to place frozen balls in oil.
– Cook 3 minutes, but watch carefully; if they are overcooked, they will fall apart.

YIELDS 35 BALLS

35

MACARONI, CHEESE AND EGG CASSEROLE

1 cup macaroni
2 cups milk
1 cup soft bread crumbs
2 tablespoons butter
2 teaspoons onion, minced
2 teaspoons parsley, minced
6 eggs, beaten
2 teaspoons salt
2 cups American cheese, grated

– Preheat oven to 325 degrees.
– Boil macaroni in lightly salted water until tender then drain.
– Mix together all ingredients except the bread crumbs.
– Put macaroni in buttered 2-quart casserole then pour mixed ingredients over macaroni and top with bread crumbs.
– Bake in oven, covered, approximately 1 1/2 hours.

SERVES 4

36

Double Macaroni and Cheese

8 ounces elbow macaroni, cooked
1 1/2 cup cheddar, shredded
1 package creamed cottage cheese (12 ounces)
1/4 cup flour
1/4 cup butter or margarine
2 cups milk
1/2 teaspoon salt
1/8 teaspoon white pepper

– Alternate layers of macaroni, cottage cheese, and cheddar in a greased 2-quart baking dish.
– Melt 1/4 cup butter and stir in flour to make a smooth mixture.
– Blend in milk gradually and heat to boiling and stir constantly.
– Cook until thickened about 2 minutes and add salt and pepper.
– Pour over macaroni and cheese.
– Bake at 375 degrees for 30-35 minutes.

Serves 4

37

FRIED MACARONI AND CHEESE

8 ounces medium or sharp cheddar cheese, grated
2 cups dry elbow macaroni, cooked and drained
1/2 teaspoon table salt
1/4 teaspoon black pepper
1/8 teaspoon paprika (optional)
3 large fresh eggs (room temperature), beaten
2 tablespoons butter, melted
1 tablespoon oil or bacon drippings

– Grate cheese of choice and set aside.
– Boil in salt water 2 cups dry elbow macaroni until tender and drain.
– Place in a large bowl and season with salt, black pepper and paprika.
– In a medium bowl, beat eggs until light and pale yellow.
– In a large skillet over low heat, heat oil and butter together.
– Quickly mix together macaroni, grated cheese and beaten eggs.
– Add mixture to skillet and stir and fry until brown and crispy.

SERVES 4-6

38

FRIED MACARONI AND CHEESE II

2 cups elbow macaroni or shells
3 eggs
1 cup cheese of your choice

– Cook macaroni in boiling salt water and drain.
– Place in a large bowl and mix in eggs and cheese until combined.
– Heat a small amount of oil in a skillet and add the macaroni mixture and fry until crisp and brown with the cheese melted and the eggs cooked thoroughly.

SERVES 4

39

Greek Lasagna Using Macaroni and Cheese

2 pounds uncooked elbow macaroni
2 pounds ground beef
1 medium onion, chopped
1 cup grated Parmesan cheese
1 package feta cheese (4 ounces)
2 cans diced tomatoes (8 ounces)
2 teaspoons ground cinnamon
salt and pepper to taste
3 cups milk
3 tablespoons cornstarch
1/4 cup butter

– Boil macaroni in lightly salted water until tender then drain. Set aside.
– Preheat the oven to 350 degrees.
– Cook ground beef and onion in a large skillet over medium-high heat until beef is evenly browned.
– Remove from heat, and drain grease.
– Stir in the tomatoes, feta cheese, Parmesan cheese, and cinnamon, then mix in macaroni and transfer to a large baking dish.
– In a saucepan over medium heat, mix together the milk and cornstarch until smooth.
– Add butter, then boil for 1 minute, remove from heat, and pour the sauce over the mixture in the baking dish.
– Bake for 1 hour in the oven, until the top is golden brown.

Serves 6

40

GOLDEN BROWN MACARONI AND CHEESE

6 cups water
1/2 teaspoon salt
2 cups uncooked elbow macaroni
4 tablespoons (1/2 stick) butter or margarine
2 1/2 cups grated mild cheddar cheese, divided
2 large eggs
1/2 cup milk
paprika, for the top

– Preheat the oven to 350 degrees. Grease an 8-inch-square baking pan.
– In a 6-quart pot, bring the salt water to a boil.
– Add the macaroni and cook until tender and drain.
– Return the macaroni to the pot and stir in the butter or margarine until melted.
– Add 2 cups of the cheddar cheese.
– In a medium bowl, beat the eggs then add in the milk.
– Add the milk mixture to the pot with the macaroni then mix it.
– Spoon it into the prepared baking pan.
– Sprinkle the remaining 1/2 cup cheddar cheese on top and dust with paprika.
– Bake, uncovered, for 30 minutes or until the cheese has melted and the casserole is warm throughout.

SERVES 5-6

⊔‖

HAM AND MACARONI BAKE WITH BROCCOLI

2 cups uncooked elbow macaroni
3 tablespoons butter or margarine
1/4 cup all-purpose flour
1/4 cup finely chopped green onion
1 teaspoon salt
1/2 teaspoon dried mustard
1/8 teaspoon pepper
2 1/2 cups milk
1 package frozen chopped broccoli, cooked, drained (about 1 1/2 cups)
2 cups cubed cooked ham
1 cup shredded sharp cheddar cheese
1/2 cup dry bread crumbs tossed with 1 tablespoon melted butter

– Boil macaroni in lightly salted water until tender then drain. Set aside.
– In a medium saucepan, melt 3 tablespoons butter over low heat.
– Add flour, green onion, salt, mustard, and pepper and stir until smooth.
– Gradually stir in milk until blended then bring to a boil, stirring constantly until mixture is thickened and bubbly.
– Stir in broccoli, macaroni, ham, and cheese.
– Transfer mixture to a 2-quart casserole and sprinkle buttered bread crumbs over ham and macaroni casserole.
– Bake at 350 degrees for 30 minutes or until golden brown.

SERVES 6

42

HAM AND MACARONI AND CHEESE

2 tablespoons butter
1 1/2 tablespoon flour
1 cup milk
1 cup grated American cheese
2 cups cooked macaroni
1/2 teaspoon salt
1 to 1 1/2 cups cooked, diced ham
2 tablespoons horseradish
2 teaspoons prepared mustard

– Cook macaroni in boiling salt water and drain.
– In a large saucepan over medium-low heat, melt the butter.
– Stir in the flour until a smooth paste is formed and gradually mix in the milk.
– Continue cooking, stirring, until it begins to bubble and thicken.
– Add cheese, macaroni and salt then mix well.
– Pour into buttered casserole dish.
– Combine remaining ingredients and sprinkle over the top of the macaroni, pressing into the mixture lightly.
– Bake at 350 degrees about 20 minutes.

SERVES 4

43

Ham (Skillet-Fried) Macaroni and Cheese

2 cups water
1/2 cup sliced celery
1/2 cup chopped onion
1/4 cup chopped green bell pepper
1 chicken bouillon cube or equivalent base or granules
1/2 teaspoon dry mustard
1 package macaroni and cheese dinner mix (about 7 1/2 ounces)
1/2 cup milk
2 cups leftover cooked cubed ham

– In a skillet, combine water, onion, celery, green pepper, bouillon, dry mustard, and macaroni portion of macaroni and cheese dinner mix.
– Bring to a boil then reduce heat, cover, and simmer, stirring occasionally, until macaroni is tender.
– Stir in the cheese sauce mix from the macaroni and cheese dinner mix.
– Stir in the milk and ham and keep covered until mixture is heated through.

Serves 4

Hamburger Macaroni and Cheese

1 cup uncooked macaroni
1/2 pound ground beef
1 onion, chopped
3/4 cup tomato sauce
1/2 can cheddar cheese soup

– Preheat oven to 400 degrees.
– Boil macaroni in lightly salted water until tender then drain.
– Fry ground beef and onions until browned and drain.
– Add tomato sauce to the beef mixture then simmer for 10 minutes.
– Lightly grease the 1-quart casserole dish.
– Spoon into the casserole dish 1/3 of meat mixture then add the macaroni.
– Add the rest of meat mixture then apply the cheese soup over top.
– Cover and bake until bubbly.

SERVES 4

45

Homemade Macaroni and Cheese

2 tablespoons butter
1/2 cup flour
4 cups milk
1 large box Velveeta
2 cups macaroni

– Preheat oven to 350 degrees.
– At medium heat, melt 2 tablespoons of butter then add 1/2 cup of flour.
– Slowly add milk to make a paste.
– Turn down to medium-low then add 3/4 of the box of Velveeta cut into small cubes and melt.
– Boil 2 cups of macaroni in salt water until tender then add it to the mix.
– Bake at 350 degrees for 30 minutes.

Serves 4

46

HOT DOG CASSEROLE

2 cups macaroni
1 tablespoon margarine
8 hot dogs
1/2 cup chopped onion
1 can Mexican-style corn (12 ounces)
1 can tomato sauce (15 ounces)
1/2 teaspoon chili powder
1 cup American cheese, diced

– Preheat oven to 350 degrees.
– Boil macaroni in lightly salted water until tender then drain. Set aside.
– Melt butter in pan then add sliced hot dogs and chopped onion.
– Cook until lightly browned then add corn (undrained), tomato sauce, and chili powder.
– Simmer for 10 minutes then add cooked macaroni and cheese.
– Bake in casserole dish and put in oven for 20-30 minutes until bubbly.

SERVES 4

47

Hot Dog Casserole II

2 packages dry macaroni and cheese (14 ounces)
1 loaf processed cheese food, cubed (1 pound)
1 package hot dogs, sliced (16 ounces)
2 cups frozen green peas, thawed
1 onion, chopped
2 cans condensed tomato soup (10.75 ounces each)
1 can condensed cream of celery soup (10.75 ounces)
1/2 teaspoon garlic powder
salt and pepper to taste

– Boil macaroni in lightly salted water until tender then drain.
– Preheat oven to 350 degrees.
– Stir in the cubed cheese, hot dogs, peas, onion, condensed tomato soup and condensed celery soup.
– Season with garlic powder, salt and pepper.
– Spread into a 9x13-inch baking dish and cover.
– Bake in the oven for 40 to 45 minutes.

Serves 8

48

IT IS SUPERB MACARONI AND CHEESE

3/4 pound bacon
1/4 cup butter or margarine
1 1/2 cup unseasoned bread crumbs
1 pound elbow macaroni
3-5 scallions, chopped
1 1/2 pounds Swiss cheese

– Preheat oven at 350 degrees.
– Cook the bacon until it is very crisp then blot dry.
– Put the butter in a small frying pan and heat at a low temperature until it's melted.
– When melted, add the bread crumbs and lightly cook until the bread crumbs are browned, stirring frequently to avoid burning the crumbs.
– Boil macaroni in lightly salted water until tender then drain into a colander.
– While the macaroni is cooking, grate the cheese and chop the scallions.
– Put a layer of macaroni on the bottom, then cheese, then crumble the bacon, then apply scallions on top.
– Make the layers thin to try and get 3 or 4 layers of pasta/cheese/bacon.
– Top with the bread crumbs and bake for 20 minutes or until the bread crumbs are slightly browned and the cheese is melted.

SERVES 6

ਖ਼ਿ

"IMITATION CHEESE" SAUCE

1 box macaroni (discard the cheese mix)
2 cups water
1/4 cup tomatoes
1/4 cup raw almonds
1/4 teaspoon garlic powder
1/2 teaspoon onion powder
1/2 tablespoon sea salt
1/2 tablespoon fresh lemon juice
2 tablespoon corn starch
1/4 cup nutritional yeast

– Boil macaroni in lightly salted water until tender then drain. Set aside.
– Blend all the ingredients until they are very smooth.
– Pour in 2-quart saucepan and cook on medium heat until thick, mixing constantly. Pour on the macaroni.

SERVES 4

50

ITALIAN MACARONI AND CHEESE

5 tablespoons butter or margarine, divided
3 tablespoons flour
1/2 teaspoon salt
1/2 teaspoon pepper
1/4 teaspoon ground nutmeg
2 1/4 cups milk
8 ounces medium pasta shells, cooked, drained
1 cup POLLY-O ricotta cheese
1 package POLLY-O Pizza Shreds 4 Cheese Blend (8 ounces)
1 tomato, sliced
1/4 cup dry bread crumbs
1/4 cup POLLY-O grated Parmesan cheese
2 tablespoons chopped fresh parsley

– Melt 3 tablespoons of the butter in large saucepan on low heat.
– Stir in flour and seasonings and cook and stir 2 minutes or until bubbly.
– Gradually stir in milk until mixed.
– Cook on medium heat until mixture boils and thickens, stirring constantly.
– Reduce heat to low. Simmer 5 minutes.
– Pour sauce over shells in large bowl then add ricotta cheese and mix lightly.
– Spoon 1/2 of the pasta mixture into 2-quart casserole then sprinkle with 1 1/2 cups of the pizza shreds.
– Cover with remaining pasta mixture and pizza shreds and top with tomato slices.

– Toss bread crumbs, Parmesan cheese, remaining 2 tablespoons butter, melted, and parsley until well mixed. Sprinkle over tomatoes.
– Bake at 350 degrees for 20 to 25 minutes or until thoroughly heated.

SERVES 4

51

IT TAKES YOUR WHOLE DAY
MACARONI AND CHEESE

8 ounces elbow macaroni
4 cups shredded sharp cheddar cheese
1 can evaporated milk (12 ounces)
1 1/2 cups milk
2 eggs
1 teaspoon salt
1/2 teaspoon ground black pepper

– In a large pot, cook the macaroni in boiling salt water until tender and drain.

– In a large bowl, mix the cooked macaroni, 3 cups of the sharp cheddar cheese, evaporated milk, milk, eggs, salt, and pepper.

– Transfer to a slow cooker or Crock-Pot that has been coated with nonstick cooking spray.

– Sprinkle with the remaining 1 cup of shredded sharp cheddar cheese.

– Cover and cook on low for 5 to 6 hours, or until the mixture is firm and golden around the edges.

– Do not remove the cover or stir the mixture until the mixture has finished cooking.

SERVES 6

52

KICKING UP DAISIES MACARONI AND CHEESE

1 1/2 cups rotelle macaroni
4 tablespoons butter, divided
1/4 cup all-purpose flour
3 cups whole milk
1 teaspoon dry mustard
3/4 teaspoon salt
1/2 teaspoon ground white pepper
3 teaspoons hot pepper sauce
1 cup shredded pepperjack cheese
1 1/2 cups shredded sharp cheddar cheese
1/2 cup grated Parmesan cheese
1/3 cup dry bread crumbs
2 teaspoons chili powder

– Bring a large pot of lightly salted water to a boil then cook the macaroni until it is tender. Drain.
– In a large saucepan over medium heat, melt 2 tablespoons butter then mix in flour and cook, stirring for 1 minute.
– Gradually mix in milk, mustard, salt, pepper and hot sauce then bring to a slow boil while stirring for 1 minute.
– Remove from heat and mix in pepperjack, cheddar and Parmesan until smooth.
– Stir in cooked pasta and pour into shallow 2-quart baking dish.
– Melt remaining 2 tablespoons butter and stir in bread crumbs and chili powder and sprinkle over macaroni mixture.
– Bake 375 degrees for 30 minutes.

SERVES 6

53

Mexican-Style Macaroni and Cheese

1 1/2 pounds lean ground beef
2 tablespoons dried onion flakes
2 packages dry macaroni and cheese (7.25 ounces each)
15 ounces nacho cheese dip
1 cup medium salsa
1 can diced green chiles (7 ounces)

– In a medium skillet over medium-high heat, cook beef with onion flakes until beef is browned then drain.
– In a large saucepan, cook the macaroni and cheese in salt water until it is tender.
– Stir in the meat and onion mixture, nacho cheese dip, salsa and green chiles.
– Reduce heat and simmer 15 minutes.

SERVES 8

54

Macaroni and Cheese with Mustard and Worcestershire Sauce

1/2 pound small elbow macaroni (about 2 cups)
2 tablespoons (1/4 stick) butter
2 1/2 cups (packed) grated extra-sharp cheddar cheese (10 ounces)
2 5-ounce cans evaporated milk
3 large eggs
1 tablespoon prepared mustard
1 teaspoon Worcestershire sauce
1/8 teaspoon cayenne pepper

– Preheat oven to 350 degrees.
– Butter 8x8x2-inch baking dish.
– Boil macaroni in lightly salted water until tender then drain.
– Add butter and toss until it is melted.
– Mix in 2 cups cheddar cheese then beat milk, eggs, mustard, Worcestershire sauce, and cayenne pepper in medium bowl to blend.
– Stir egg mixture into macaroni and transfer to the prepared dish.
– Sprinkle remaining 1/2 cup cheddar cheese over top.
– Bake macaroni until golden on top for 1 hour.

Serves 6

55

Macaroni and Cheese with Prosciutto

8 ounces small elbow macaroni (2 cups)
1 1/2 cups (packed) grated Gruyère cheese (about 6 ounces)
1 cup whipping cream
1 cup whole milk
3 ounces thinly sliced prosciutto, coarsely chopped
3 tablespoons grated Parmesan cheese
1/8 teaspoon ground nutmeg

– Preheat to 400 degrees.
– Butter 11x7-inch baking dish.
– Boil macaroni in lightly salted water until tender then drain.
– Mix 1/2 cup Gruyère, cream, milk, prosciutto, Parmesan and nutmeg in large bowl.
– Add macaroni and combine with the previous mixture.
– Season with salt and pepper.
– Transfer to the prepared baking dish.
– Sprinkle remaining 1 cup Gruyère over the dish and bake for 20 minutes until the cheese melts and macaroni and cheese sets.

Serves 6

56

My Sister-in-Law's Macaroni and Cheese

4 cups cooked elbow macaroni, drained
2 cups grated cheddar cheese
3 eggs, beaten
1/2 cup sour cream
4 tablespoons butter, cut into pieces
1/2 teaspoon salt
1 cup milk

– Preheat oven to 350 degrees.
– Boil macaroni in lightly salted water until tender then drain and place in a large bowl.
– While still hot, add the cheddar.
– In a separate bowl, combine the remaining ingredients and add to the macaroni mixture.
– Pour macaroni mixture into a casserole dish and bake for 30 to 45 minutes.
– Top with additional cheese if desired.

Serves 6

57

Mustard Seasoning Macaroni and Cheese

3/4 cup butter
3/4 cup flour
4 cups milk
2 cups chicken broth
1/2 teaspoon ground nutmeg
cayenne pepper
dry mustard
salt
white pepper
3 cups grated cheddar cheese
1 cup grated Gruyere or Swiss cheese
1/2 cup grated Parmesan cheese
1 pound macaroni, cooked and drained
1 1/2 cups croutons

– Melt butter in large skillet over medium-low heat.
– Stir in flour to make a light paste, cooking and stirring 2 to 3 minutes.
– Add milk and broth. Simmer 6 to 8 minutes until thickened and liquid has evaporated.
– Season to taste with nutmeg, cayenne, mustard, salt and pepper.
– Combine cheeses and stir 3/4 of cheese mix into the sauce.
– Pour cheese sauce over cooked macaroni, then into 13x9-inch baking dish.
– Sprinkle evenly with remaining cheese. Crush croutons and sprinkle evenly over top.
– Bake at 350 degrees until cheese melts and browns lightly, 35 to 45 minutes.

Serves 6

58

NASSAU MACARONI AND CHEESE

2 packages dry macaroni and cheese (7.25 ounces each)
1 green bell pepper, chopped
1 onion, chopped
1 large tomato, chopped
1 pound bacon, cooked and crumbled

– Preheat the oven at 350 degrees.
– Boil macaroni in lightly salted water until tender then drain.
– In a large bowl, mix together the chopped bell green pepper, onion, tomato, and crumbled bacon.
– Mix in prepared macaroni and cheese to large bowl with vegetables and bacon.
– Stir gradually to mix ingredients evenly.
– Pour into a 9x13-inch baking dish.
– Bake in an oven for 45 to 60 minutes, or until crispy on top.

SERVES 8

59

New Orleans Macaroni and Cheese

1 package elbow macaroni (8 ounces)
1 cup Andouille sausage, diced
4 tablespoons butter
3/4 cup bread crumbs
1/2 cup grated Parmesan cheese
1 onion, chopped
2 stalks celery, chopped
1 tablespoon all-purpose flour
1/2 teaspoon paprika
1/2 teaspoon prepared mustard
1 1/2 cups milk
1 cup grated Gruyere cheese
1 1/2 cups shredded cheddar cheese
kosher salt to taste
black pepper to taste

– Boil macaroni in lightly salted water until tender then drain.
– In a small pan, cook the Andouille sausage over medium heat until done. Set aside.
– In the same pan, melt 1 tablespoon butter over medium heat. Then add bread crumbs and stir to coat.
– Cool, and then mix in Parmesan and set aside.
– In a medium saucepan, melt 1 tablespoon butter. Lightly cook onions and celery until transparent and transfer to a bowl.
– In the same saucepan, melt 1 tablespoon butter over medium heat.
– Mix in the flour to make a white light paste, keeping care not to let it brown.

– Mix in paprika and mustard, then mix in milk and bring to boil over medium heat.
– Add Gruyere and cheddar cheeses then let it simmer for 10 minutes, stirring often, until thick enough to coat the back of a spoon.
– Season with salt and pepper to taste.
– Preheat the oven to 350 degrees.
– Butter a 9x13-inch pan, or similar-sized casserole dish, and transfer cooked macaroni to the dish, then add the Andouille sausage.
– Stir in the cheese mixture and sprinkle the bread crumb and Parmesan mixture evenly over the top.
– Bake for 20 minutes or until crust turns golden brown.

SERVES 6-8

6◑

NUKED MACARONI AND CHEESE

1 cup elbow macaroni
1 cup milk
3 tablespoons all-purpose flour
salt and pepper to taste
2 tablespoons butter
1 cup shredded cheddar cheese

– Boil macaroni in lightly salted water until tender then drain. Set aside.
– In a microwave-safe bowl, combine milk, flour, salt and pepper to taste and mix until smooth.
– Add butter and cheese and microwave on high for 5 minutes and mix again until it is smooth.
– Microwave for an additional 4 to 5 minutes and mix once again to ensure that it is smooth and no lumps remain.
– Add cooked pasta to mixture. Stir and serve.

SERVES 5

61

No-Brainer Macaroni and Cheese

2 1/4 cups boiling water
1/2 stick butter
2 cups uncooked macaroni
1 pound small curd cottage cheese
8 ounces Velveeta cheese

– Preheat the oven at 375 degrees.
– Bring water and butter to a boil.
– Combine with uncooked macaroni, cottage cheese, and Velveeta cheese.
– Stir well and carefully pour into a baking dish.
– Bake in the oven for 45 minutes, stirring occasionally.

Serve 6

62

Old-Fashioned Macaroni and Cheese

1 1/2 cups elbow macaroni
4 tablespoons butter, divided
1/4 cup flour
3 cups milk
1 teaspoon dry mustard
3/4 teaspoon salt
1/4 teaspoon freshly ground pepper
1 pinch ground red pepper
1 1/2 cups shredded sharp cheddar cheese
1/4 cup freshly grated Parmesan cheese
1/3 cup plain dry bread crumbs

– Preheat oven to 375 degrees.
– Boil macaroni in lightly salted water until tender then drain and rinse under cold water.
– Meanwhile, melt 2 tablespoons butter in large saucepan over medium heat.
– Stir in flour and cook, stirring for 1 minute, then gradually mix in milk, mustard, salt and peppers and bring to boil, mixing for 1 minute.
– Remove from heat and whisk in cheeses until melted and smooth and stir in drained macaroni.
– Pour into shallow 2-quart baking dish.
– Melt remaining 2 tablespoons butter, stir in bread crumbs and sprinkle over macaroni.
– Bake 30 minutes

Serves 4-6

63

OLD-FASHIONED MACARONI AND CHEESE II

1/2 pound macaroni
1 cup cheese chips
3 tablespoons butter
1 teaspoon salt
1/8 teaspoon cayenne pepper
1/2 cup milk
1 egg
1/2 cup buttered bread crumbs

– Boil macaroni in lightly salted water until tender then drain and rinse in cold water.
– Cover bottom of baking dish with layer of macaroni, a sprinkle of cheese, bits of butter, salt and pepper.
– Continue until all is used, having cheese on top.
– Mix milk and egg together, pour over the dish, cover top with crumbs.
– Bake in a preheated oven at 350 degrees until the top is browned.

SERVES 4

64

PAN-FRIED MACARONI AND CHEESE

1/2 cup butter
2 cups uncooked elbow macaroni
1/4 cup minced onion
2 tablespoons minced green pepper
1 teaspoon salt
1/4 teaspoon dry mustard
2 cups shredded cheddar cheese

– Melt butter in medium heated skillet.
– Add uncooked macaroni, onion, green pepper, salt and dry mustard.
– Stir in 2 cups water and bring to boil.
– Reduce heat to low and let simmer covered until the macaroni is tender.
– Stir occasionally.
– Remove from heat and stir in shredded cheese.

SERVES 4

65

Pepper Ham Macaroni and Cheese

1 package elbow macaroni (8 ounces)
5 tablespoons butter
5 tablespoons all-purpose flour
1 quart warm milk (110 degrees F/45 degrees C)
salt and pepper to taste
1 pinch cayenne pepper
1/4 pound cubed ham
5 ounces cheddar cheese, cubed
5 ounces mozzarella cheese, cubed
5 ounces Monterey Jack cheese, cubed
paprika to taste

– Preheat oven to 350 degrees.
– Grease a 9x13 baking dish.
– Bring a large pot of lightly salted water to a boil.
– Boil macaroni in lightly salted water until tender then drain.
– In medium saucepan, melt butter and stir in flour to make a paste.
– Cook 1 to 2 minutes, stirring constantly, then mix in warm milk gradually to make a white sauce.
– Bring to a boil, then reduce heat and simmer.
– Mix in salt, pepper, and cayenne, and stir frequently until sauce thickens.
– Remove pan from heat and stir in cheddar, mozzarella, jack and ham.
– Combine pasta with sauce and stir well, then pour into baking dish.
– Sprinkle paprika on top and bake 45 to 60 minutes.

Serves 4-6

66

RED PEPPER SAUCE MACARONI AND CHEESE PIE

2 cups shredded cheddar cheese
1 cup uncooked macaroni
2 1/4 cups milk
4 eggs
1/2 cup Bisquick
1/4 teaspoon salt
1/4 teaspoon red pepper sauce
1/4 cup shredded cheddar cheese

– Heat oven to 400 degrees.
– Grease 10x1 1/2-inch pie plate.
– Mix the macaroni and cheese and sprinkle in the pie plate.
– Mix the remaining ingredients, except 1/4 cup cheese, until smooth, 15 seconds in blender on high or 1 minute with hand beater.
– Pour into the pie plate and bake 40 minutes.
– Sprinkle with 1/4 cup cheese and bake until the cheese is melted, 1 to 2 minutes.

SERVES 4

67

Baked Pepperoni with Macaroni and Cheese

3 cups uncooked elbow macaroni
2 cans tomato sauce (8 ounces each)
2 cans tomato paste (6 ounces each)
1/2 pound shredded cheddar cheese
1/2 pound shredded sharp cheddar cheese
25 slices pepperoni sausage
salt and pepper to taste
onion powder to taste
garlic powder to taste

– Preheat oven to 350 degrees.
– Boil macaroni in lightly salted water until tender then drain.
– In a 9x13-inch baking dish, combine cooked macaroni, tomato sauce, tomato paste, cheeses, pepperoni, salt, pepper, onion powder and garlic powder.
– Bake in preheated oven for 45 minutes.

Serves 6-8

68

Pineapple and Ham Macaroni and Cheese

1/2 pound elbow macaroni, uncooked
1 jar processed cheese or processed cheese sauce (Cheez Whiz)
1 1/2 cups chopped cooked ham
1 can crushed pineapple, well drained (8 ounces)
1/2 cup finely chopped green peppers
1/4 cup finely chopped onions

– Boil macaroni in lightly salted water until tender then drain.
– Stir in cheese sauce until well coated.
– Add all of the remaining ingredients and serve immediately.

Serves 4-6

69

SALSA AND THE MARIACHI BAND
MACARONI AND CHEESE

3 1/2 cups macaroni, cooked and drained
1 3/4 cups low-fat sharp cheddar cheese, shredded
1/2 cups onion, finely chopped
3 tablespoons chopped parsley
1 3/4 cups low-fat cottage cheese
1/2 cup evaporated skim milk
2 teaspoons Dijon-style mustard
1 slice bread, crumbled
3 tablespoons grated Parmesan cheese
1/2 cups salsa
1 teaspoon fajita seasoning
salt and pepper

– Preheat oven to 350 degrees.
– In a large bowl, combine cooked macaroni, cheddar cheese, onion, and parsley.
– In a blender or food processor, combine cottage cheese, milk, and mustard.
– Process until smooth then mix in salsa and fajita seasoning and pour over macaroni mixture.
– Mix thoroughly and add salt and pepper to taste.
– Coat a 2-quart casserole dish with nonstick cooking spray and place macaroni mixture into dish.
– Sprinkle bread crumbs and Parmesan cheese over casserole and bake for 20 minutes.

SERVES 6-8

70

SAUCY SAUSAGE MACARONI AND CHEESE

1 pound mild Italian sausage or ground beef
1/4 cup chopped green or red bell pepper
1/4 cup chopped onion
2 cups dry small elbow macaroni
2 cups water
1 cup evaporated milk
1 cup chili sauce
1/2 cup shredded cheddar cheese

– Cook sausage, bell pepper and onion in large skillet until sausage is no longer pink then drain.
– Stir in macaroni and water.
– Cook, stirring occasionally, until the mixture comes to a boil. Cover, then reduce heat to low.
– Stir occasionally until pasta is tender.
– Stir in evaporated milk and chili sauce.
– Remove from heat then sprinkle with cheese.
– Let stand for 5 minutes or until cheese is melted.

SERVES 6

71

Slap/Dash Macaroni and Cheese

1 package elbow macaroni (7 ounces)
1 tablespoon butter
2 cloves garlic, minced
1 pinch cayenne pepper
1 tablespoon all-purpose flour
1 cup canned evaporated skim milk
1/4 teaspoon salt
1 1/4 cups shredded low-fat cheddar cheese

– Boil macaroni in lightly salted water until tender then drain.
– Meanwhile, melt butter in a medium sauce pan.
– Add garlic and cayenne pepper and cook 1 minute over medium heat.
– Add the flour and cook 1 minute, stirring constantly, then add the milk and salt and bring to a simmer, stirring frequently.
– Simmer 2 minutes, reduce heat to low, and stir in 1 cup cheese.
– Drain pasta and add it to the sauce and cook for 1 minute.
– Sprinkle with remaining 1/4 cup cheese before serving.

Serves 4

72

STROGANOFF MACARONI AND CHEESE

1 can Healthy Request cream of mushroom soup (10.75 ounces)
1 1/2 cups shredded Kraft low-fat cheddar cheese (6 ounces)
1/2 cup sliced mushrooms, drained
1/3 cup nonfat sour cream
1 teaspoon dried parsley flakes
1/4 teaspoon black pepper
2 cups hot cooked elbow macaroni, rinsed and drained

– Preheat oven to 350 degrees.
– Spray an 8x8-inch baking dish with nonstick spray.
– In a medium saucepan, combine mushroom soup and cheddar cheese.
– Cook over medium heat until cheese melts, stirring constantly, and remove from heat.
– Stir in mushrooms, sour cream, parsley flakes, and black pepper then add macaroni and mix well.
– Pour mixture into prepared baking dish and bake for 30 minutes.

SERVES 4

73

Soy Macaroni and Cheese

8 ounces macaroni (or another pasta of your choice)
2 tablespoons soy margarine (or other dairy-free margarine)
2 tablespoons flour
1 cup soy milk
4-8 ounces soy cheddar cheese
additional soy milk
salt (optional)

– Cook macaroni in boiling water, according to package directions.
– While the pasta is boiling, melt margarine in a medium saucepan over medium heat.
– Add flour until bubbly.
– Slowly add 1 cup soy milk.
– Bring to a boil, stirring constantly (a whisk works well).
– If the sauce does not thicken, add another tablespoon of flour.
– If using cheese that is not already shredded, grate cheese.
– Add slowly, stirring until the sauce thickens and you get the consistency you desire.
– Add more soy milk if mixture gets too thick while stirring in the cheese.
– Add salt, if desired.
– Drain cooked pasta and mix in cheese sauce

Serves 4

74

SUBTLE MACARONI AND CHEESE

5 ounces extra-sharp cheese, grated
1 3/4 cups elbow macaroni
5 ounces extra-sharp cheddar cheese, cubed
1 2/3 tablespoons flour
1 1/2 teaspoons salt
1 1/2 teaspoons dry mustard
1/4 teaspoon ground pepper
1/8 teaspoon cayenne
1/8 teaspoon ground nutmeg
1 1/3 cups half and half
1 1/3 cups whipping cream
2/3 cup sour cream
2 large eggs
3/4 teaspoon Worcestershire sauce

– Preheat oven to 350 degrees.
– Lightly butter 9x13x2-inch glass baking dish.
– Cook macaroni in boiling lightly salted water until tender then drain.
– Transfer to the prepared dish.
– Mix in cubed cheese. Mix flour, salt, mustard, black pepper, cayenne pepper and nutmeg in medium bowl until smooth.
– Gradually mix in half and half, then whipping cream and sour cream.
– Add eggs and Worcestershire sauce and mix together.
– Pour over macaroni mixture and mix.
– Sprinkle grated cheese over it.
– Bake macaroni and cheese until just set around edges, but sauce is still liquid in center, for approximately 25 minutes.

SERVES 4

75

Spicy Macaroni and Cheese

1 1/2 cups uncooked elbow macaroni
6 tablespoons butter
1/4 cup flour
1 1/2 teaspoons salt
dash ground cayenne pepper
2 cups milk
8 ounces shredded sharp cheddar cheese
6 eggs, separated

– Boil macaroni in lightly salted water until tender then drain. Set aside.
– Melt butter over medium heat in a large saucepan.
– Blend in flour, salt and peppers and stir well.
– Gradually add milk, stirring constantly until thickened.
– Remove from heat and add cheese, stirring until cheese is melted.
– Beat egg yolks until light then quickly stir into cheese sauce.
– Mix macaroni with cheese sauce.
– In a separate bowl, beat egg whites until stiff and fold into macaroni mixture.
– Transfer mixture to a 3-quart casserole.
– Bake at 475 degrees for 10 minutes.
– Reduce heat to 400 degrees and bake 25 minutes longer.

Serves 6

76

SPICY MACARONI AND CHEESE—
JUST DONE DIFFERENTLY!

1 package elbow macaroni (8 ounces)
5 tablespoons butter
5 tablespoons all-purpose flour
1 quart warm milk (110 degrees F/45 degrees C)
salt and pepper to taste
1 pinch cayenne pepper
1/4 pound cubed ham
5 ounces cheddar cheese, cubed
5 ounces mozzarella cheese, cubed
5 ounces Monterey Jack cheese, cubed
paprika to taste

– Preheat oven to 350 degrees. Grease a 9x13 baking dish.
– Boil macaroni in lightly salted water until tender then drain.
– In medium saucepan, melt butter and stir in flour to make a paste.
– Cook 1 to 2 minutes, stirring constantly, then mix in warm milk gradually to make a white sauce.
– Bring to a boil, then reduce heat and simmer.
– Mix in salt, pepper, and cayenne. Stir frequently until sauce thickens.
– Remove pan from heat and stir in cheddar, mozzarella, jack and ham.
– Combine pasta with sauce and stir well.
– Pour into baking dish and sprinkle paprika on top.
– Bake 45 to 60 minutes or until top is crisp.
– Let rest 20 minutes before serving.

SERVES 4-6

77

MACARONI AND CHEESE SOUP

1 package uncooked macaroni and cheese (14 ounces)
1 cup chopped broccoli
1/2 cup chopped onion
1 cup water
2 1/2 cups milk
1 can condensed cream of cheddar cheese soup (11 ounces)
1 cup cubed cooked ham

– Boil macaroni in lightly salted water until tender then drain. Set aside.
– In a medium saucepan, combine broccoli, onion and water.
– Bring to a boil and cook until the broccoli is tender.
– Stir in macaroni, cheese mixture from package, milk, soup and ham.
– Return to a boil briefly for 3-4 minutes.

SERVES 6

78

Macaroni and Cheese Soup II

1 1/2 tablespoons soy margarine or canola oil
1 large onion, finely chopped
2 medium celery ribs, finely diced
1 can great northern bean, drained and rinsed
3 1/2 cups vegetable stock or water
1/2 pound mushrooms, coarsely chopped
1 1/2 teaspoons salt-free herb and spice seasoning mix
1 cup soy milk or low-fat milk (or as needed)
1 1/2 cups cheddar-style soy cheese or firmly packed grated low-fat
    cheddar cheese
2 cups small pasta (such as shells or elbows)
salt
1 dash cayenne pepper

– Heat the margarine or oil in a soup pot.
– Add the onion and celery and lightly cook over medium-low heat
until the onion is golden.
– Puree the beans until smooth (add a small amount of water if
necessary).
– Cover the onions and celery with water until it is just covering them.
– Bring to a simmer then stir in the bean puree, mushrooms, and
seasoning mix.
– Simmer gently, covered for 30-35 minutes.
– Stir in the milk or soy until almost a thick consistency.
– Remove from the heat and sprinkle in the cheese, gradually stirring
each time until it is well melted and set aside.

– Boil macaroni in lightly salted water until tender then drain and stir into the soup.

– Adjust the consistency of the soup with more milk or soy as needed, then return to a low heat.

– Season to taste with salt and cayenne.

SERVES 6

79

Swiss Cheese and Ham Macaroni and Cheese

1/4 cup unsalted butter
5 tablespoons all-purpose flour
2 cups whole milk
salt
white pepper
1 pinch ground nutmeg
8 ounces dry elbow macaroni, uncooked
8 ounces domestic Swiss cheese, grated
8 ounces ham, cubed
1 cup frozen baby peas, thawed
1/4 cup grated Parmesan cheese

– Preheat oven to 350 degrees.
– In a 2- to 3-quart saucepan, melt butter over medium heat.
– Add the flour and stir for 2 minutes, slowly adding the milk, mixing to combine.
– Bring to a simmer. Add the salt, white pepper and nutmeg.
– Reduce the heat to low and let sauce simmer slowly for 20 minutes.
– Boil macaroni in lightly salted water until tender then drain. Set aside.
– Remove the sauce from the heat, add the Swiss cheese and stir until it melts.
– Combine the sauce, cubed ham and peas with the drained macaroni.
– Pour the macaroni mixture into a greased 11x8x2-inch dish.
– Sprinkle the Parmesan cheese on top and bake in preheated oven for 25 minutes.

SERVES 6

Taco Casserole

1 pound lean ground beef
8 ounces macaroni
1/2 cup chopped onion
1 can condensed tomato soup (10.75 ounces)
1 can diced tomatoes (14.5 ounces)
1 package taco seasoning mix (1.25 ounces)
2 ounces shredded Cheddar cheese
2 ounces shredded Monterey Jack cheese
1 cup crushed tortilla chips
1/2 cup sour cream
1/4 cup chopped green onions

– Preheat oven to 350 degrees.
– Boil macaroni in lightly salted water until tender then drain.
– In a large skillet, cook and stir ground beef and chopped onion over medium heat until it is browned.
– Mix in tomato soup, diced tomatoes, and taco seasoning mix then stir in the macaroni.
– Spoon beef mixture into a 9x13-inch baking dish and sprinkle crumbled taco chips and grated cheese on top.
– Bake for 30 to 35 minutes, until the cheese is melted.
– Serve with chopped green onions and sour cream.

SERVES 6-8

81

Tangy Macaroni and Cheese

1 1/2 cups uncooked elbow macaroni
6 tablespoons butter
1/4 cup flour
1 1/2 teaspoons salt
dash ground cayenne pepper
2 cups milk
8 ounces shredded sharp cheddar cheese
6 eggs, separated

– Boil macaroni in lightly salted water until tender then drain.
– Melt butter over medium heat in a large saucepan.
– Blend in flour, salt and peppers while stirring well.
– Gradually add milk, stirring constantly.
– Continue cooking and stirring until thickened, then remove from heat and add cheese, stirring until cheese is melted.
– Beat egg yolks until light then quickly stir into cheese sauce.
– Mix macaroni with cheese sauce.
– In a separate bowl, beat egg whites until stiff then fold into macaroni mixture.
– Transfer mixture to a 3-quart casserole dish.
– Bake at 475 degrees for 10 minutes then reduce heat to 400 degrees and bake 25 minutes longer.

Serves 6

82

Tex-Mex (And Closer to the Border) Macaroni and Cheese

1 pound ground beef
1 teaspoon salt
1/8 teaspoon ground black pepper
1 green bell pepper, chopped
1 medium onion, chopped
1 package macaroni and cheese dinner, prepared with milk and margarine as package directs
1 can tomatoes, diced, with liquid (14.5 to 16 ounces)
1 can whole kernel corn, drained (12 ounces)
1 can tomato paste (6 ounces)

– Brown ground beef with salt and pepper in a large skillet.
– Add onion and green pepper and continue cooking until onion is tender.
– Add corn, tomatoes and tomato paste and heat through.
– Stir in prepared macaroni and cheese dinner then let it simmer for 8 to 10 minutes

Serves 4-6

83

TEX-MEX MACARONI CHEESE

1 pound lean ground beef
1 package taco seasoning mix (1.25 ounces)
1 package white Cheddar macaroni and cheese mix (7.3 ounces)

– In a large skillet, brown beef and drain off excess fat.
– Add taco seasoning and water according to seasoning package directions and simmer for 10 minutes or until liquid is absorbed then set aside.
– Boil macaroni in lightly salted water until tender then drain.
– Combine beef mixture and macaroni and cheese.
– Mix together and serve.

SERVES 6

84

THICK AND CREAMY MACARONI AND CHEESE

3 cups spiral-shaped pasta
2/3 cup milk
1 pound Velveeta cheese, cubed
1/4 teaspoon dry mustard
1/2 teaspoon ground turmeric
salt and pepper to taste

– Boil macaroni in lightly salted water until tender then drain.
– While cooking the macaroini, put remaining ingredients in the top of double boiler over simmering water.
– Stir until it is smooth.
– Keep cheese mixture warm till pasta is cooked and drained.
– Stir pasta into cheese.

85

Tomato Red Macaroni Salad

1 pound elbow macaroni, cooked, drained and cooled
1 green pepper, diced small
1 onion, diced
3-4 stalks celery, sliced small (up to one cup can be used)
1 cup fresh tomato, diced
1 cup cucumber, diced
1 cup oil
3/4 cup brown sugar
1/2 cup lemon juice
3/4 cup ketchup

– In large mixing bowl, combine your macaroni, pepper, onion, celery, tomato, and cucumber.
– In another bowl, mix the oil, brown sugar, lemon juice and ketchup.
– Pour sauce over the macaroni and vegetables.
– Mix and chill.

Serves 6

86

MACARONI AND CHEESE WITH TOMATOES

8 ounces elbow macaroni
2 ripe tomatoes, sliced
2 tablespoons butter
1 tablespoon flour
1/4 teaspoon dry mustard
1/2 teaspoon salt
2 cups skim milk
2 cups grated cheddar cheese
1/2 cup fresh bread crumbs

– Boil macaroni in lightly salted water until tender then drain.
– Preheat oven 375 degrees.
– Grease the casserole dish with butter.
– Slice tomatoes into 1/2-inch-thick slices and set aside.
– Crumble bread crumbs with fingertips and set aside.
– In a 2-quart saucepan over medium heat, melt the butter and add flour, dry mustard and salt.
– Cook together for 2 or 3 minutes.
– Add milk gradually and continue stirring until mixture thickens then add cheese and stir until melted.
– Place 2 tomato slices in bottom of casserole dish.
– Add half of the macaroni.
– Place another 2 tomato slices, then the remainder of macaroni.
– Pour sauce over all the casserole.
– Add 3 slices tomato on top and sprinkle with bread crumbs.
– Bake 20 minutes until it is golden and cooked through.

SERVES 6

87

FAMILY TUNA CASSEROLE

1 can tuna, drained
8 ounces elbow macaroni
4 tablespoons butter
3 tablespoons finely chopped onion
2 tablespoons finely chopped green bell pepper
2 tablespoons all-purpose flour
3/4 teaspoon salt or seasoned salt
1/8 teaspoon pepper
1 cup milk
1/2 cup frozen peas, thawed
1 can cream of mushroom soup
1 cup shredded cheddar cheese
buttered soft bread crumbs

– Cook macaroni until tender, drain and rinse.
– Melt butter in a large saucepan.
– Add chopped onions and bell pepper and lightly cook over low heat for 3 minutes.
– Add flour, salt and pepper and stir until smooth and bubbly.
– Add milk and mushroom soup and stir over low heat until smooth and thickened.
– Add cooked macaroni, flaked tuna, peas and half of the cheese to sauce mixture while stirring constantly.
– Pour mixture into 2-quart buttered casserole then sprinkle remaining cheese then buttered bread crumbs.
– Bake at 350 degrees for 30 to 40 minutes or until nicely browned.

SERVES 4-6

MACARONI AND WHITE CHEESE

1 pound macaroni
1 cup chopped onion
1 tablespoon butter
1 cup sliced mushrooms
3 cloves minced garlic
1 cup grated extra old white cheddar cheese
1 cup grated Gouda cheese
1 cup grated Gruyere
1 cup grated Asiago cheese
2 cups hot cream
2 tablespoons Dijon mustard
1/2 cup grated Romano cheese

– Preheat the oven to 400 degrees.
– Lightly cook together the onion, butter and mushrooms until browned.
– Add the minced garlic and lightly cook for one minute and set aside.
– Boil macaroni in lightly salted water until tender then drain and set aside.
– Add to the pasta the hot cream and the Dijon mustard and stir well.
– Add the cheddar, Gouda, Gruyere, Asiago and the mushroom mixture to the pasta and stir well.
– Turn mixture into a well-buttered 3-quart baking dish.
– Top with Romano (or with the remaining other cheeses).
– Bake in the oven for 25 minutes or until hot.

SERVES 6

89

Vegan Macaroni and No Cheese

8 ounces uncooked elbow macaroni
1 tablespoon vegetable oil
1 medium onion, chopped
1 cup cashews
1/3 cup lemon juice
1 1/3 cups water
salt to taste
1/3 cup canola oil
4 ounces roasted red peppers, drained
3 tablespoons nutritional yeast
1 teaspoon garlic powder
1 teaspoon onion powder

– Preheat oven to 350 degrees.
– Boil macaroni in lightly salted water until tender then drain and transfer to a medium baking dish.
– Heat vegetable oil in a medium saucepan over medium heat.
– Stir in onion and cook until tender and lightly browned. Gently mix with the macaroni.
– In a blender or food processor, mix cashews, lemon juice, water, and salt.
– Gradually blend in canola oil, roasted red peppers, nutritional yeast, garlic powder, and onion powder and blend until it is smooth.
– Thoroughly mix with the macaroni and onions.
– Bake 45 minutes in the oven or until lightly browned.

Serves 4

90

Vegan Macaroni and No Cheese II

1/2 cup nutritional yeast flakes
1/2 cup white flour or wheat flour
1/2-1 teaspoon salt
1-2 teaspoons garlic powder or 2-3 cloves garlic, chopped
1/4 teaspoon paprika (optional)
2 cups soy milk
1/4 cup margarine or oil
1/2 teaspoon prepared mustard or mustard powder
8 ounces elbow macaroni, cooked and drained

– Boil macaroni in lightly salted water until tender then drain. Set aside.
– Mix dry ingredients in a saucepan then add the milk.
– Cook over medium heat, mixing constantly, until it thickens and bubbles.
– Cook and stir 30 seconds more, then remove from the heat.
– Mix in the margarine and mustard.
– Add more milk or water if mixture is too thick.
– Add macaroni and mix well

SERVES 4

९१

Macaroni and "Vegi-Cheese"

2 cups of macaroni
1 tablespoon soy non-hydrogenated vegan margarine
1 tablespoon flour
3 cups vegan soy milk
4 ounces "Soymage" cheddar cheese substitute
1 small clove garlic, minced
1 medium onion, chopped
1 tablespoon minced parsley
1 teaspoon salt
1 teaspoon white pepper
paprika

– Boil macaroni in lightly salted water until tender then drain. Set aside.
– Melt margarine in a saucepan. Add flour then slowly add the soy milk, constantly mixing.
– If the consistency is not thick enough, slowly sprinkle in some flour, starting with 1/2 tablespoon and adding more if necessary.
– Add cheese, garlic, onion, parsley, salt, and pepper and mix until sauce is thick and smooth.
– Combine sauce and pasta, and sprinkle with paprika.
– Bake at 375 degrees in a greased casserole dish for at least 30 minutes.

Serve 4

92

Nice and Simple
Macaroni and "Vegi-Cheese"

1 or 2 slices of soy cheese
1 large box of a good vegetable or fake chicken
elbow macaroni

– Spray nonstick cooking spray in a pot then place the noodles in the pot.
– Put in enough broth so that the noodles are partially submerged.
– Boil the noodles in the broth while stirring in the slices of cheese.
– Add more broth and more cheese and basically cook it until the noodles are done, and there is no more broth and it is cheesy enough for your taste.
– The broth and the cheese will form a sauce and be thick.

Serves 3

93

Cheesy Vegan Macaroni and "Cheese"

2 cups vegan soy milk
4 ounces pimentos
1 1/2 teaspoons salt
1/2 teaspoon onion powder
3 tablespoons yeast flakes
1/4 teaspoon garlic
2 tablespoons cornstarch
1/4 cup raw cashews
1 tablespoon lemon juice
16 ounces egg-free macaroni noodles

– Blend cashews and pimentos in soy milk until smooth.
– Add the remaining ingredients and cook in a heavy saucepan until thick, stirring constantly at medium heat.
– While preparing the cheese sauce, cook the bag of egg-free macaroni noodles.
– Drain noodles and pour the cheese sauce over noodles. Mix well and serve.

Serves 4-6

Vegetarian Tex-Mex Macaroni

1 1/2 cups macaroni
1 can crushed tomatoes
1 can baked beans in tomato sauce
1/4 cup Bulls-Eye vegan BBQ sauce
2 tablespoons ketchup
1 tablespoon taco seasoning
sprinkling of crushed chili peppers

– Boil macaroni in lightly salted water until tender then drain.
– Add the crushed tomatoes, baked beans, the vegan BBQ Sauce, ketchup, taco seasoning and chili peppers.
– Let it simmer on medium low heat while stirring constantly.

Serves 2

95

West Coast Macaroni and Cheese

1/2 cup unsalted butter, divided into 1/4 cups
1 medium onion
1/4 cup all-purpose flour
2 cups milk, warmed
2 cups half and half, warmed
3 tablespoons honey mustard
2 teaspoons Worcestershire sauce
4 1/2 cups extra-sharp cheddar cheese, shredded and divided
3 1/2 cups and 1 cup (or any combination) of your favorite cheeses
kosher salt
fresh pepper
cayenne pepper
1 pound macaroni
1 1/3 cups seasoned dry bread crumbs or fresh bread crumbs

– Boil macaroni in lightly salted water until tender then drain.
– Preheat oven to 400 degrees.
– Butter a 9x13 baking dish.
– Melt 1/4 cup butter in a large saucepan over medium heat.
– Add onion and lightly cook for 3 minutes.
– Stir in flour and stir for 3 minutes.
– Mix in milk and the half and half, stirring and cooking for 6 minutes or until slightly thickened.
– Stir in mustard and Worcestershire sauce and remove from heat.
– Stir in 3 1/2 cups cheese until it is melted, then season with salt, pepper and cayenne to taste.
– Place half of cooked macaroni into baking dish. Pour in half of sauce, mixing well.

– Add rest of macaroni and mix in the remaining sauce.
– Top with remaining 1 cup of cheese and bake for approximately 20 minutes.
– Melt the remaining 1/4 cup butter in a large skillet over medium heat. Add bread crumbs, stirring until lightly toasted.
– Remove dish from oven and sprinkle crumbs on top.
– Bake until crumbs are golden brown

SERVES 4-6

96

MACARONI AND "TOFU CHEESE"

1 box macaroni, cooked
1 medium onion, finely diced
1 cup (or more) of mashed tofu
1 1/3 cups vegan soy milk
2 tablespoons flour
1/2 cup nutritional yeast
1 dash vegan Worcestershire sauce
3 dashes tamari sauce
1/2 teaspoon garlic powder
pepper to taste
soy Parmesan

– Preheat oven to 375 degrees.
– Boil macaroni in lightly salted water until tender then drain. Set aside.
– While macaroni is boiling, chop onion then combine soy milk, flour, yeast, Worcestershire sauce, tamari sauce, pepper and garlic powder.
– Put drained macaroni in an oblong baking dish.
– Add tofu and soy milk mixture.
– Shake soy Parmesan on top and mix.
– Bake for approximately 30 minutes.

SERVES 4

97
WILD MUSHROOM GRATIN WITH MACARONI AND CHEESE

1/2 pound elbow macaroni
2 quarts water, salted to taste
1/2 pound oyster mushrooms, chopped
1/2 pound shiitake mushrooms, chopped
1/2 pound chanterelle mushrooms, chopped
4 cloves garlic, finely chopped
3 shallots, finely chopped
4 tablespoons olive oil
1 tablespoon chopped chives
1 tablespoon chopped parsley
1/4 pound coarsely grated cheese, Swiss or Parmesan

– Boil macaroni in lightly salted water until tender then drain and rinse in cold water. Set aside.

– While macaroni is cooking, mix mushrooms together with garlic and shallots in olive oil until golden brown for 3 or 4 minutes, then add chives and parsley.

– Toss drained macaroni with lightly cooked mushrooms and arrange in an oven-safe dish.

– Bake in a preheated 350-degree oven for about 10 minutes, stirring occasionally, until mixture is heated through.

– Sprinkle with cheese, broil for 1 or 2 minutes, just until cheese is melted and browned.

– Serve immediately.

SERVES 4

98

Vegan Macaroni and Cheese (With Kick!)

1 1/2 cups macaroni
2 tablespoons nutritional yeast
1/3 cup original vegan soy milk (I use low fat)
1 tablespoon soy non-hydrogenated vegan margarine (I use Earth Balance)
2 soy/tofu American cheese slices
salt and pepper to taste

– Boil macaroni in lightly salted water until tender then drain and set aside.
– While macaroni is sitting in colander, mix soy milk and nutritional yeast in the pan.
– Return macaroni to pan and mix.
– Salt and pepper to taste and then add the two slices of cheese.
– Turn burner on to assist in melting the cheese and stir until cheese is melted.

SERVES 4

୧୧

Vegetables with Macaroni and Cheese

1 cup macaroni
2 medium carrots, thinly sliced
1 cup frozen peas
1/3 cup milk
2 tablespoons cream cheese
1/2 teaspoon dried basil
1/2 cup shredded part-skim mozzarella OR cheddar cheese
1 tablespoon freshly grated Parmesan cheese
1 green onion, chopped
salt and pepper

– Boil macaroni in lightly salted water until tender then drain.
– Meanwhile, steam or boil carrots for 4 minutes then add peas and cook until carrots are tender-crisp for approximately 3 minutes.
– Drain and return to the pot.
– In small saucepan, heat milk over medium heat, until steaming.
– Mix in cream cheese until smooth then stir in basil.
– Add to pasta along with vegetables, cheeses and green onions.
– Mix then season with salt and pepper to taste.

Serves 4

100

What's-His-Name Chicken and Macaroni

2 cups macaroni
2 cups diced, cooked chicken meat
2 cups shredded cheddar cheese
1 can condensed cream of chicken soup (10.75 ounces)
1 cup milk
1 can sliced mushrooms (4.5 ounces)

– Boil macaroni in lightly salted water until tender then drain.
– Preheat oven to 350 degrees.
– In a large bowl, combine cooked macaroni, chicken, cheddar cheese, soup, milk and mushrooms then place mixture in a 9x13-inch baking dish.
– Bake in the oven for 50 to 60 minutes then serve.

Serves 4-6

🞖

Wisconsin Macaroni and Cheese

1 1/3 cups elbow macaroni
1 slice whole wheat bread
2 tablespoons (1/4 stick) butter
2 tablespoons all-purpose flour
3/4 cup low-fat milk
3/4 cup canned vegetable broth
2 green onions, thinly sliced
1 1/2 cups packed grated sharp cheddar cheese

– Preheat the oven to 350 degrees.
– Boil macaroni in lightly salted water until tender then drain.
– Meanwhile, grind bread in processor to fine crumbs and transfer to small bowl.
– Melt butter in medium saucepan then mix 1/2 tablespoon into crumbs.
– Add flour to remaining butter, mixing over medium heat 2 minutes.
– Gradually mix in milk and broth then bring to boil, mixing constantly.
– Add green onions then mix 2 minutes longer.
– Remove from heat then add cheese and stir until melted.
– Mix macaroni into sauce.
– Season to taste with salt and pepper.
– Spoon into 9-inch pie plate and sprinkle crumbs over it.
– Broil in the oven until crumbs brown, about 2 minutes, and serve.

SERVES 4-5

Printed in the United States
99386LV00003B/103/A